Seasons

What Can You See in Summer?

Siân Smith

Heinemann LIBRARY

Chicago, Illinois

© 2015 Heinemann Library
an imprint of Capstone Global Library, LLC
Chicago, Illinois

Edited by James Benefield and Kathrn Clay
Designed by Richard Parker
Picture research by Tracy Cummins
Production by Helen McCreath
Originated by Capstone Global Library Ltd

Library of Congress Cataloging-in-Publication Data
Cataloging-in-publication information is on file
with the Library of Congress.
ISBN 978-1-4846-0355-0 (paperback)
ISBN 978-1-4846-0366-6 (eBook PDF)

Photo Credits

Dreamstime.com: Tramper2, 18; Getty Images: ChristopherBernard,
17, back cover, karelnoppe, 7, Peter Cade, 6, 22 (right); Shutterstock:
ayosphoto, 20 (middle), djgis, 4, ER_09, 9, Franck Boston, 20 (right),
Im Perfect Lazybones, 12, LilKar, 13, 22 (left), Mihai Simonia, 14, miker,
15, Monkey Business Images, 5, MoreenBlackthorne, cover, Pavel L
Photo and Video, 20 (left), Poznyakov, 19, Richard Schramm, 11, 21,
Rob Marmion, 10, Subbotina Anna, 16, wavebreakmedia, 8

Contents

Things You Can See in Summer

You can see the Sun.

You can see sun hats.

sunscreen

You can see **sunscreen**.

You can see sunglasses.

You can see picnics.

You can see strawberries.

You can see watermelon.

You can see ice cream.

You can see sunflowers.

You can see **butterflies**.

You can see thunderstorms.

You can see carnivals.

You can see hot dogs.

You can see lemonade.

You can see swimming pools.

You can see sandcastles.

Summer Quiz

Which clothes would you wear in summer?

The four seasons follow a pattern. Which season comes after summer?

spring

summer

winter

?

Picture Glossary

 **butterflies**

 **sunscreen**

Index

Answer to quiz on page 20: sunglasses and swimsuits
Answer to question on page 21: fall

Notes for Teachers and Parents

Before Reading

Building background: Talk about the seasons of the year. Which season are we in at the moment? Ask children what they would see if they looked out a window in summer.

After Reading

Recall and reflect: Which season is before summer? Which season follows summer? What is the weather like in summer? What is the best thing about summer?

Sentence knowledge: Help children count the number of words in each sentence.

Word knowledge (phonics): Look at the word *can* on any page. Ask children to think of words that rhyme with *can*. (fan, man, pan, ran, plan)

Word recognition: Have children point to the word *see* on page 5. Ask children to find the word *see* on other pages.

Extending Ideas

Make a Paper Plate Sun: Give each child a white paper plate. Tell them to color the back of the plate yellow and glue it to a larger piece of blue paper. Then they should draw around their hands on bright yellow paper and cut out the hand shapes. Next they should stick their hand shapes around the outline of the Sun to represent the Sun's rays. When finished, have children think of words to describe the Sun. (e.g. hot, round, yellow, etc.)

In This Book

Topic Words
butterflies
carnivals
hot dogs
ice cream
lemonade
picnics
sandcastles
strawberries
sun
sunflowers
sunglasses
sun hats
sunscreen
swimming pools
thunderstorms
watermelons

Topic
Summer

High-frequency Words
a
can
see
you

Sentence Stem
You can see _____.

Ask Children to Read These Words:
picnic   p. 8
ice cream   p. 11
sunflowers   p. 12